Transported by the Lion of Judah

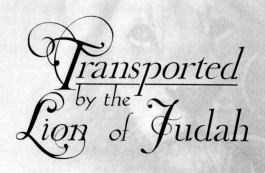

by Anne Elmer

"Experience first hand this amazing account as Jesus, the Lion of Judah, transports a lonely hospital-bound woman from her place of infirmity into a nearly worldwide trip to finally see the Church, and many outside the Church—through the eyes of Jesus Himself. Prepare to have your view of 'The Church' changed forever, and I mean it!"

—Steve Shultz, The Elijah List

Transported by the Lion of Judah

by Anne Elmer

Published by Elijah List Publications, LLC
Albany, Oregon

Transported by the Lion of Judah
Copyright © 2003 by Anne Elmer
Second Edition, 2007
Second Printing, August 2008
Third Printing, February 2010

Distributed by Elijah List Publications, LLC

International Standard Book Number: 978-1-938311-13-0

Published by
Elijah List Publications, LLC
528 Ellsworth St. SW
Albany, Oregon 97321 USA
www.elijahlist.com

Cover design: Shelly Holbert

Unless otherwise indicated, all Scripture quotations are from the HOLY BIBLE, NEW INTERNATIONAL VERSION, copyright © 1973, 1978, 1984 International Bible Society. Used by permission of Zondervan.

Printed in the United States of America.

ENDORSEMENTS

"Anne Elmer's riveting series of divine visitations by the Lion of Judah are nothing short of phenomenal. Having heard her account first-hand several times, I am still undone each time I hear it. Now published, readers will find these visitations C. S. Lewis-ian in cadence and symbolization, and yet deeply personal and enormously relevant for the Body of Christ today. Anne's own life—born in Britain and transplanted by design to a village near Versailles—is an open book of integrity and servant hood which make an endorsement of this publication a joy and privilege. Ride along with Anne on the back of the King as He takes you to churches around the world, removing veils, freeing hearts and minds, and convicting the cold-hearted. I guarantee you will fall in love with Him all over again."

Teresa Neumann
Albany, Oregon

"I was riveted as I read this true story. Anne's story of her visitations from the Lion of Judah is awesome. The lessons she learned on the trips the Lion took her on have changed my perspective on many things—especially concerning the Church and judging God's people. I would recommend this book to young and old alike. You will love it!"

Derene Shultz
Albany, Oregon

"Anne, and her husband, Malgwyn, are true servants of the Lord. Their loving-kindness and humbleness have greatly impacted my life. When I heard this account first-hand from Anne, and then later reading about it, my life has been touched. My perspective of the Father has really changed, including about His love for me and for the Church. You will truly get a deeper revelation of the Lion of Judah, the almost unbelievable kindness of the Father, and His patience and goodness towards each person on earth—both the saved and the unsaved. And yet, in the midst of His kindness, He is still Almighty, Powerful, and Sovereign. This story demonstrates that everything happens according to HIS will and His PERFECT timing. Be prepared to be encouraged, have your 'God perspective' changed, and to have your love grow!"

Tawny Shultz
Albany, Oregon

"I really enjoyed this and appreciated the 'HEART' of Anne's journey as she traveled and soared with the

Lion of Judah, Jesus Christ. I often experience the Lord in similar ways, and it was very refreshing to hear of her profound and amazing adventures. This is a great read and helps to demonstrate how actively the Lord is at work in all of our lives. Anne gives us a unique look and insight at the *creative beauty* of our Lord and Savior, Jesus Christ. What really impacted my heart was Chapter Seventeen—*The Working Christian*. I actually got a little teary eyed over this part:

'Jesus: But Christian, if you had come with Me, we could have flown together, and you could have sown your seeds from a great height where the Holy Spirit would have carried them and planted them in good soil, in ground that I have already prepared. And if you had flown with Me you would have been refreshed and renewed, and not so tired now. Ah well, maybe tomorrow!'

Hmm, I wonder how many times the Lord has said that to me. I find that often in our Christian lives, myself included, we get too busy to do 'God Stuff' and forget to spend quality intimate time with our Creator. Sometimes the Lord just wants us to delight in Him as He delights in us. I think the Lord likes to have fun with us as we soar in prayer, praise, and worship, but He also likes to go play with us as well. I often take long hikes with the Lord where we walk, talk and laugh together. In fact, the Lord has given me some amazing prophetic words during these times spent with Him. And oh, by the way, I usually have a divine appointment or two along the trail ways where the Lord will divinely intervene in someone's life. I always come away renewed, strengthened, and energized through these wonderful times spent with the Lord. The *joy* of the Lord is truly our strength!

Well, I think I am about due for another hike. Thanks Anne, and keep up the great work! I look forward to hearing more of your times spent with the Lion of Judah."

Lisa Cooke Doyle
Vancouver, Washington

"Transported by the Lion of Judah is truly a prophetic word from the Lord to the Body of Christ for today. Don't take off on a 'rabbit trail' by trying to determine whether or not Anne Elmer was actually transported, or you'll miss the powerful message the Lord will give you through this book.

This book has helped me, more than any other, to see and understand the love the Lord has for people as He looks at their hearts and motives. God is so much less rigid and more tolerant than I have seen Him or than the Church has taught Him to be—and certainly more than I have learned to be. *Transported by the Lion of Judah* has brought me into repentance of my own intolerance and rigidness of other denominations and people in general, who are seeking God. I was surprised to see how much hardness I had in my heart. Being a 'good Christian' for many years, I knew it was wrong to be unloving to people in other denominations and outside the Church—I had only deceived myself. I will never look upon people the way that I have in the past—praise God! Through the renewing of my mind, I have seen a more loving God than I have ever known Him to be. As the time nears for Christ to return for His Bride without spot or blemish, He is calling us to obey His command, to truly love one another as He loves us."

Carol Ruda
Salem, Oregon

Transported by the Lion of Judah

Contents

Preface		13
CHAPTER 1	The Background	17
CHAPTER 2	Annonay	21
CHAPTER 3	Spirals on the Wall	25
CHAPTER 4	Learning to Laugh	33
CHAPTER 5	The Dying Lady	39
CHAPTER 6	Falling in Love	45
CHAPTER 7	The First Journey	51
CHAPTER 8	Picnics	55
CHAPTER 9	The Igloo Church	59
CHAPTER 10	Across the World	63
CHAPTER 11	The Roaring Lion	67
CHAPTER 12	Non-Christian Gatherings	73
CHAPTER 13	The Pride Problem	77
CHAPTER 14	Walking and Dancing	81
CHAPTER 15	More About Annonay	85
CHAPTER 16	The "Whys and Wherefores"	89
CHAPTER 17	The Working Christian	95
CHAPTER 18	The Last Word	99
To Contact Anne & Malgwyn Elmer		103

PREFACE

I was born in a small industrial town in Lancashire, brought up to go to church on Sunday mornings and Sunday school in the afternoons. It was our parish church, part of the Church of England. I didn't know it then, but I do now, that the "Church of England" can include anything from "low" to "high!" That means there is a wide spectrum of ways of worshipping. Some are very plain and simple, and some very Roman Catholic in style. The type of church depends on the traditions and preferences of the minister in charge at the time.

My church was of the "low" variety, which meant that they had very little decoration in the form of brass candlesticks and gold crosses, and the services included a minimum of ritual. There was a great emphasis on evangelism, and from time-to-time there were pulpit thumping sermons on being "born again." My own family didn't agree with these outbursts and had a particular objection to the expression being "born again." They assured me that it was sufficient to go to church, say your prayers every evening, and be a "good girl!"

There was an active youth group, and in-spite of the differing ideas between home and church, I became an active member—although I believe I was too pious at times and gave my family a hard time by becoming *religious*.

Through further education and on into my marriage, I continued to be an active member of the local Anglican Church wherever I was living, carrying a certain amount of my religiosity with me. Although I must say, I was as sincere as I knew how to be.

In 1983, the Lord intervened dramatically in the life of our family. At that time we had three children, aged 14, 13, and 7, and had moved to France, where we became members of St. Mark's Anglican Church in Versailles. There we met people who talked about Jesus as though He sat down to supper with them. It was then we recognized just how little we knew the Lord personally. And our relationships with Him as individuals, as well as in the family, have been growing ever since.

Thanks must go to St. Mark's and the many friends we have from there who helped us on our journey. We had a lot of fun learning together during the 15 years we were part of that congregation.

In 1998, the Lord pushed us out of the English community where we were so comfortable, and into the Eglise Eau-Vive in Boulogne-Billancourt, where we are now elders. Thanks go to the members there for their patience with our stumbling French, and for the way they allow and encourage us to be who the Lord has called us to be.

I also want to thank my husband, children, and grandchildren for their love and inspiration.

And last, but by no means least, the Lord Jesus Christ, the Lion of Judah, without whom there would be no story!

—Anne Elmer

CHAPTER 1

The Background

I have a friend who talks to the Lord all the time! I mean really—all the time. They have conversations like I have with my husband, or a neighbor, or a friend. He tells her what she must watch on the television, and then who on the program He wants her to pray for! He takes her down certain streets just to show her things! And all of this is in the real world, just a part of her daily life.

She is a middle aged widow and has lived "alone" for many years, so maybe it's easier for her than me. I live with my husband, and together we have a gift of hospitality, so our house is rarely empty and usually full to overflowing with people from all over the world. What a blessing that is! And yes, the Lord talks to us too, but nevertheless, I have to confess to a certain amount of jealousy regarding my friend's closeness with the Lord. Maybe you know lots of people like that, but I don't.

And certainly the number of people I know who hear directly from the Lord are increasing as He extends the prophetic voice on the earth—but I know few people who hold continual conversations with their Savior as my friend does!

I often told the Lord that I was jealous, in a nice sort of way of course, and that I would like to hear His voice as she did. I know that He deals with each of us as individuals, and what He wanted to do with my friend may not be what He wanted to do with me. The way He chose to talk to her, may not be the way He chose to talk to me. But I also know that if we delight in Him, He will give us the desires of our hearts (see Psalm 37:4). Please note that I am not recommending that you seek voices or visions, but just to seek Him and His closeness, and let Him deal with you as He wants, revealing Himself to you in the way He knows is best for you.

Well, He answered this particular desire in a way I was not expecting at all! The result of my prayers was that I got sick, very sick, and had to be hospitalized for an emergency operation, far away from home where no one could visit. As He kept me hidden away in this "secret place" for three weeks, He revealed Himself to me in a way I could not have imagined. He walked with me, and talked with me, and showed me amazing things that He is doing all over the world. He taught me things I had not previously had the time, or maybe the inclination to learn. But most important of all, He showed me how passionately He loves me, and how desperate He is for me to love Him. I feel like I had the same privilege as

Moses when He was hidden in the cleft of the rock and the Lord let all His goodness pass in front of him!

"And the LORD said, 'I will cause all My goodness to pass in front of you, and I will proclaim My name, the LORD, in your presence...'"—Exodus 33:19

I hope that what follows does not seem irreverent, as though I just think of the Lord as a friend, but in the same way that He showed Moses only His goodness at that particular time, so He hid me away to show me His love—an amazing, overwhelming, passionate love. It was a life changing experience, as it was for Moses, and many can testify to the new level of serenity in my life. I have an absolute confidence that the Lord is in control of everything—absolutely everything.

During the year which followed these experiences, a lot of people told me that I should write a book, but I never felt it was right. Now I feel that it is the time and all the Glory must go to the Lord!

CHAPTER 2

Annonay

My husband, Malgwyn, and I had spent Christmas with some of the family in Provence, in the South of France, and had decided to leave early and meander slowly back to Paris, by taking "normal" roads and not the motorway. It takes much longer, but is so much more beautiful, and we knew we would find a small hotel in an "off the beaten track" place to spend a night on the way. So there we were in the middle of nowhere, just my husband and I, appreciating the beauty of France and reflecting on the good Christmas we had celebrated, when my gallbladder started to bother me! I had already seen a specialist at home because it had been causing minor problems for some time, but the doctor had said that it wasn't urgent. And we had prayed for healing and were expecting the stones I knew I had, to be dissolved away by the Holy Spirit!

When the pain started, our first reaction was to pray, but as the evening wore on we had to admit that we needed a doctor. The local doctor came out to the hotel, and because of a strike of ambulance workers, he took me to the hospital in his own car. My husband followed up hill and down dale, over very icy roads the doctor obviously knew well and consequently took quite fast, while all the time my husband was wondering if he would ever be able to find the hotel again! We had specially chosen an out-of-the-way place.

Anyway, the end of this part of the story is that I was admitted to a hospital in a small town in the Ardeche, called Annonay. A beautiful place nestled in the center of several river valleys surrounded by mountains and famous for just one thing—the Montgolfier brothers, who lived there and had designed the first hot air balloon.

The doctors in Annonay Hospital tried to calm things down in order to send me back home for treatment, but my gallbladder refused, and on my third day there I had to have an emergency operation to have it removed! That was the first day the Lord really spoke to me, although, even before He did I had been at total peace. My husband had returned to Paris to spend New Year's with the children and grandchildren, knowing that I was in the Lord's hands. I was! Here's what He said when He first spoke to me:

"Now Anne, I have brought you to this place. This is Annonay. It's an *anonymous* place, and you too are anonymous here, because I want to teach you some things."

I cannot tell you whether it was an audible voice or just a voice in my spirit, but I had no doubt at all that I was hearing Him and it seemed the most natural thing in the world!

Malgwyn and I thought it was we who had chosen this out-of-the-way place, but obviously it was God who had done that. Not only had He chosen it for us, but it looked as though He had named it too, with a name that worked as a play-on-words in both English and French!

I knew that had I been hospitalized near home, I would have had lots of visitors, very little rest, and certainly no time with the Lord like I was about to experience. How often do we try to pray our way out of problems and take authority over demonic situations, when all the time God is saying, "Quit blaming the devil! It's Me—God!"

Lord give me more discernment!

I do not want to argue the theology here, but I do want to make the point that my family and I believe in divine healing. I am not one to preach that the Lord uses sickness to teach us things. I think it happens often, but it is not what God wants! If I had been prepared to go on retreat, or to shut myself away with Him for three weeks, He would have taught me these things anyway! But like so many of us, I want the Lord to bless me, change me, and minister to me without giving Him the time to do what I ask. We live in an "instant" world, and expect instant answers to prayer. So sometimes the Lord has to move in unpredictable ways to give us what we desire, and more important, what He desires.

He was about to show me what He desired.

CHAPTER 3

Spirals on the Wall

So, I found myself recovering from an emergency operation to take away my gallbladder, in a hospital bed in the small mountain town of, Annonay. Because of severe pain and a total lack of energy, I often lay unmoving in bed, with eyes closed or just looking at the wall at the bottom of the bed—and that's where the visions started!

I felt as though the spots on the wall were becoming spirals, leaping off the wall and moving towards other spirals, joining them and then rushing off out of sight. There were many different colors, even though the wall was just a dull grey with pale blue spots. What I saw made me think of modern Christmas tree lights, with different programs for flashing and colors, always changing direction, color, and sequence!

I blamed the morphine that I was taking, and each time I spoke to my husband on the phone, I asked him to get people to pray that the hallucinations would stop because I didn't like them at all. (This was another case of not recognizing when God was trying to say something. He is so patient with me!) It was as though the air was full of these spirals continually moving, and joining, and separating.

Later, I began to see other things on the wall, and one day I saw animals of every kind. There were every sort I could imagine, and they were all rushing in the same direction.

"Oh!" I exclaimed to the Lord, "It's just like Creation!"

"That's what it is," He replied. "And the spirals you see are the DNA."

Suddenly, I understood. I already knew that DNA could be represented by strips of information, a bit like on a computer tape, and here, what I was seeing were not hallucinations at all, but the real air through my spiritual eyes. The air was, and is, charged with the creative power of God. He had opened my spiritual eyes to see the air full of His creative breath. I suddenly had the explanation for many Bible stories that I had just thought of as "miracles!" Now I saw how they had happened. Yes, they were miracles of course, but they happened because of the DNA present in the air to create and rearrange things at the word of the Lord.

When Moses' staff turned into a snake and back again, it was just a "quick DNA change."

"...the LORD said to him, 'Reach out your hand and take it by the tail.' So Moses reached out and took hold of the snake and it turned back into a staff in his hand."—Exodus 4:4

When Belshazzar saw the handwriting on the wall, the hand was just created by the DNA in the air and a creative word from God.

"Suddenly the fingers of a human hand appeared and wrote on the plaster of the wall, near the lampstand in the royal palace. The king watched the hand as it wrote."—Daniel 5:5

There are stories now of the Lord doing creative miracles once more (maybe He has never stopped, but I just haven't heard about them). We have our own story of when the Lord "created" money and left it on our bedroom floor when we were staying in a friend's house in Ireland—but that's not part of this story! We also know people who have received gold teeth or silver fillings at the hand of the Lord. These situations happen because the Lord has spoken a creative word into the air which is continually charged with DNA!

What a revelation it was to me to know that the air is permanently charged with the same creative power that started the universe, and all it needs is a word from the Creator to make something new! Our God is just as ready today to create new things as He was in the seven days of Genesis!

I was so excited, and knew, that I knew, that I knew, that the whole Story is true! Second Timothy 3:16 (NAS) says, *"All Scripture is inspired by God..."*—not just the bits we like!

I have always been one who believed the whole Bible, and have never been in agreement with some people who say that we cannot be sure of the details before Genesis 11. For me, if God said it—it's true. I may not understand it all, but I can trust Him and I know His word is true!

So here I was in my hospital bed where God had promised to teach me some things, and the first thing He taught me was something I thought I already knew! About the beginning of things, and how His creative power is still available today. The reason we don't see more of it in our churches is because of the lack of belief! God has chosen, for the most part, to limit Himself to our faith.

"...According to your faith will it be done to you."
—Matthew 9:29

Many Christians are not convinced of the creation story, and consequently whether they understand the situation or not, they are denying the power of the Creator God, and limiting His freedom to work in their own lives as well as those around them. In His own town Jesus could do few miracles because of their lack of faith (see Mark 6:5).

When my husband and I have taught on the six-day creation story before, we have had the attitude, "This is what we believe—you can take it or leave it—it doesn't affect your salvation." And it doesn't! But here, for the first time, I realized just how much what I personally believe limits what God can do in my personal life, as well as in the lives of those I pray for. What a responsibility I have!

Do we really believe in a creative, miracle-working God who spoke the universe into being? If we do, and also know His love for us demonstrated in Jesus, then there is nothing He cannot do through us, and for us, and in us—absolutely nothing!

I found myself wondering if others had seen similar things under the influence of morphine, and felt that probably they had. God uses every possible way to draw men to Himself. But I was saddened by the thought that others had used what they had seen to design flashing, moving things, and to sell them for personal gain. How often do we take God's creations and use them for "commercial activities?"

The visions continued, and I felt as though I saw every invention that had ever been designed. I knew every single one of these things had come from a Creator God. I found myself repenting of the fact that we had elevated scientists and engineers and not given God the Glory for what had really been His ideas in the first place. He has been the inspiration behind every invention ever thought of. I was struck by how much we take things for granted, and began to wonder how people had dreamed up what are now every day items such as a screw, a hinge, a door handle, a hair brush, etc. I began to give praise to the Lord for every good idea that man had ever had.

I saw many things; books of every description, theater in all its different forms, electrical gadgets, different modes of transport, and I knew that everything, absolutely everything had originated with our Creator God, but that man had taken God's ideas and used them for commercial gain. I was very sad. I asked for forgiveness for the sins of man, and praised the God of Creation for His patience, love, and longsuffering!

We must learn to appreciate afresh the things which make our daily lives run smoothly, and to give the thanks and praise for everything to God the Creator. And we must believe the Bible—all of it.

I came home from the hospital convinced that my husband and I should once more teach all that we knew about creation, and encourage people to make the foundation of the world part of the foundation of their personal faith.

But for the moment, with no one to preach to, and no energy to preach or teach anyway, there I was in Annonay, with a view of the mountains and the rooftops out of my bedroom window. I shared my room with an old lady in her eighties, who was hard of hearing, had poor sight, and very few visitors, so she rarely interrupted my conversations with the Lord. I had the perfect opportunity to talk to Him freely! But of course, it was He who had created this opportunity, because He wanted to talk to me! He also wanted me to talk to the old lady, but more of that later!

CHAPTER 4

Learning to Laugh

When I had no energy to move, I just lay with eyes closed and prayed in silence, or I watched the never-ending visions on the wall at the bottom of the bed. Once I saw hundreds of eyes, but it wasn't at all scary as it might be in a film. I was aware that they were all different species, and I knew by looking at them which animal they were. I marveled at the thousands of different ways the Lord had designed and redesigned the same thing! However, there was one pair of eyes which kept coming into the vision again and again, and I knew they were lion's eyes. They were so beautiful, and soft and strong, and seemed to hold all the character of the lion. I asked the Lord why they kept coming back when all the others kept changing, and He replied that He wanted me to think about the Lion of Judah. So I did.

That meant thinking of victory, and I never doubted that He would bring me victory in the illness I was suffering at that time. As I thought about the Lion of Judah and all that meant as one of the names of Jesus, it was as though He, the Lion, came and stood at the side of my bed, and the whole hospital room was full of His presence. I felt as though if I stretched out my hand I would touch Him, but I was too scared to do that! If I touched Him and discovered that He really was there, I thought I would completely freak out. And if I didn't touch Him, because He was only "in my head," maybe I would be disappointed! I didn't really realize all that was happening at that time, but I knew something important was going on and I wanted to savor every minute!

From that time on, for the rest of my hospital stay, the Lion of Judah was my constant companion. I was aware of His presence every minute, and most of the time could see Him there in my room, laid at the side of the bed or standing at the foot of the bed.

I spent a long time thinking of songs about the Lion of Judah, and then songs about the other names of the Lord, as well as the name "Jesus," and then singing in my head the songs I knew. There were many, and I could spend quite a long time without repeating any of them. Sometimes if I was just too tired for anything else, I would repeat the name Jesus over and over and then put it to music in my mind. But then I started repeating one simple song. It was a children's song I had learned from my two-year-old granddaughter, and it goes like this:

I love you Jesus, deep down in my heart,
I'm talking about deep, deep, deep down,
Deep down in my heart!

When I got to the "deep, deep" line, the Lion of Judah changed from being majestic and victorious as He had been through the rest of my worship, and became like a pantomime lion, or like a puppet, very floppy, and He danced as though He was on strings! He made me laugh! I sang it over and over again, because I enjoyed watching Him perform for me. I began to be aware of how little I had laughed, and how much fun Jesus is, and how much fun I had missed in my life because of my "serious" attitude toward God.

Jesus, when He walked the earth, was obviously so good to be around, that hundreds of people followed Him wherever He went. And I'm sure it wasn't just because of the miracles He did, but because He was fun to be with. I was saddened for the years I had spent in "serious religion," and regretted the times I have resisted fun and laughter because of the God I thought I knew, but didn't know at all!

It's time to lay down our false images, and really get to know the Jesus of the scriptures, who was obviously a man with a sense of humor. Try reading the gospels and looking for the amusing things that happen, or that Jesus says!

We are created in God's image, and so we must have His sense of humor somewhere hidden in each of us. Satan is the one who doesn't have humor in him! He is also the one who wants to steal and destroy our God-given sense of humor. I went on to laugh a lot with the Lord, and to enjoy His presence as never before.

One day, much nearer the end of my stay in the hospital, I was sitting in the chair at the side of my bed, and I was looking at the Lion who was lying under the bed. His head was by my feet, and His rear end was sticking out and up at the other side of the bed, because He was far too big to fit in a small space! He looked like a huge bloodhound from a cartoon film! His eyes were closed, and I looked at Him with love and affection, and then I asked very quietly,

"Are you asleep?"

With a very slow, deliberate movement, and a look of mock scorn on His face, but a smile in His voice, He opened one eye and replied,

"I NEVER sleep!"

His action and voice made me laugh, and the verse which went through my head is forever printed on my memory!

"...He who watches over you will not slumber, indeed He who watches over Israel will neither slumber nor sleep."—Psalm 121:3-4

I knew once more that the Lord had brought me there to set me free from preconceived ideas, to show me how much He loved me, and how much fun it was to love Him. He was keeping guard over me, and He always would.

CHAPTER 5

The Dying Lady

We'll call the lady in the next bed, Madame Dupont. She was not well at all, and obviously had a broken hip, although I never discovered whether that was the only reason for her hospital stay. She was in her mid-eighties and had terrible bedsores from her restricted movement. Whenever the nurses came to dress her sores, she would cry, or sometimes call out to God, or sometimes swear profusely! I used to pray silently for her, and several times I asked the Lord to save her and take her home. I didn't know if she believed in Him, but I knew that He loved her, so that was the beginning of my prayers.

"Lord I know you love her and I'm asking you to have mercy on her, to save her and to let her die!"

She was of Italian origin, but had had a French husband who had died twenty-five years previously.

She was the youngest of eight brothers and sisters, and from the little that we talked, I began to understand that she had not had an easy life as a young child in the mountains in southern Italy, or as a foreign wife here in France. She had two children who telephoned regularly, but the only visitor she had in the three weeks that we shared the hospital room was her grandson, Michael, and he came only once.

Madame Dupont never seemed to know if it was day or night, and she often talked to herself, or she had long conversations with the imaginary visitors she "saw." I guess that's what I was doing too, so maybe I shouldn't be so quick to judge her as crazy!

I gathered that her grandson, Michael, was the real love of her life. She had obviously looked after him when he was young and loved him dearly. I supposed that the family had been Catholic, and this was confirmed when the priest on his Sunday rounds came and gave her Mass.

One evening the Lord told me that He was going to take her home. I immediately started to pray!

"O Lord I don't know if she knows you. I suppose You've been there somewhere in her life, but I don't want her to go to Hell. Please save her and let her go to Heaven."

There I was, launching into prayer before I knew the whole story! Will I never learn! The Lord stopped me in full flow and said, "Listen! I said I was going to take her home! That means Heaven. But I can't do that until she recognizes Me. I'm going to reveal Myself and Heaven to her. Your job is to pray that she recognizes Me!" So that's what I did! I also spent a lot of that night listening for her breathing to see if she was alive or dead.

A couple of nights later, it was three o'clock in the morning and all was quiet, when the Lord said to me, "Get up and pray for Madame Dupont."

This was not many days after I had had my operation, and getting out of bed was not the easiest thing to do. I had tubes coming in and tubes going out, quite a lot of discomfort, and no energy to go anywhere. I told the Lord all that (as if He didn't know), but the feeling wouldn't go away. So I finally called across to her, "Madame Dupont, I'm going to come and pray for you."

She didn't object, so I climbed out of my bed, took hold of the tubes and bags, and struggled across to stand by her side. I laid my hand on her head and prayed for no more than a minute or two, then said, "Amen," and struggled back to bed.

A few minutes after I had got settled again, I heard her call to me, so I said, "Yes?"

"Your son who is with you," she replied, "How old is he?"

I thought that this was one of her crazy moments, so I just said, "Twenty-four," knowing well that both my sons were a long, long way away.

"What a diamond he is!" she exclaimed.

And immediately the Lord spoke again, and said to me, "See, she doesn't recognize Me. Now pray that she will recognize Me, and then I can take her home!"

I was completely dumbfounded. Jesus had been standing at my side and I hadn't seen Him, but she had! I now saw the folly of my first prayers for her of, "Lord in your mercy, let her die."

Here Jesus was saying to me, "In My mercy, I can't let her die! She mustn't die until she recognizes Me."

I prayed for her spiritual eyes to be opened, and for her to recognize all that the Lord wanted her to see. Paul prayed for the Ephesians that they may have the Spirit of wisdom and revelation that they may know Him better (see Ephesians 1:17). Should we pray anything less for those we love? Or even for those we don't! I find myself more and more in my day-to-day life praying for the Lord to reveal Himself to everyone I meet—the baker, the butcher, the people in a restaurant, or in the traffic jam! If we don't pray for them, who will?

The following day, it seemed as though Madame Dupont had "lost" several years. She was very calm, but obviously living in a happier period of her life when her grandchildren had been around her. I realized that the Lord was taking her back to a time when she would recognize Him, maybe from something she had seen or experienced earlier in life.

A couple of nights later, she suddenly exclaimed, "Oh, look at that! It's beautiful, what a lovely place!"

I thought she was seeing Heaven and wondered if this would be her last moment, but then it turned into one of her fantasies, and she started calling for Michael to prepare the suitcases, because they were off on holiday!

As my health improved and I was able to sit up and chat, I often talked to her and prayed with her. I can honestly say that the Lord gave me His love for her, and I do look forward to meeting her again when we meet in Heaven.

I believe she died the day I left the hospital.

CHAPTER 6

Falling in Love

I come from the north of England. I was born in industrial Lancashire just after the end of the Second World War, and life was not always easy, but it was very secure. As a child I never had any occasion to doubt that I was loved and wanted, and although words of affection were rarely spoken, they were often felt! I never heard my parents say that they loved me, or each other, but neither did I doubt it. As a child I knew no divorced people. It just didn't happen in our part of the world! Neither did I hear other parents say words of love to their children. I don't think my family was exceptional in its unspoken affection, but rather it was the norm. No one ever talked of love—there was no need to. It was just understood. And anyway, to talk of it would be considered "soppy!"

I realize now that it was not only words which were missing from my early life, but also physical affection.

Hugs were for special occasions, and if you were hurt, you were loved better, anything more than that was seen as "spoiling the child." But still, I must repeat that my childhood was very secure!

It was with this same attitude that my husband and I brought up our own children. We have not gone "over the top" using words of love to each other, and we didn't "waste" words of affection on them, for that would be "soppy" and unnecessary because they had no reason to doubt that we as parents loved them, or that we loved each other. It is relatively recent that I have learned to express my affection for, not just my children, but anyone!

When we moved to France in 1983, one of the things we had to get used to was the French habit of kissing everyone each time anyone arrived or left! It was not easy for us, and was even "painful" at times, but now we can't imagine life any other way!

The words of love I didn't use with my children, I now pour over my grandchildren, encouraged by my French daughter-in-law, whose background is so different to mine and my husband's. If one of her children calls to her, she can often be heard to reply, "Oui mon amour, mon trésor, que j'aime avec tout mon coeur." (Yes my love, my treasure that I love with all my heart!)

It's just different!

Anyway, all that is the background for the next part of my visions!

One day, early on in my hospital stay, I was feeling that I hadn't slept well. Madame Dupont had shouted and cried a lot in the night, and I really felt in need of a nap. I settled down into bed and told the Lord I needed a good sleep. At once I saw a picture of a young couple with arms round each other, going for a walk in the woods. The Lord spoke, "It can be just as refreshing to go out with someone you love, as it can be to have a good nap!"

I reluctantly agreed, so He continued, "Do you want to go to sleep, or do you want to come out with Me?"

What choice did I have! I knew I could sleep later and knew I would enjoy myself "going out" with the Lord.

He began to sing to me, "Come fly with Me, come fly, let's fly away..."

It was a song I had known years before, and it was only later that I understood the true significance of what He was singing. But for the moment, I just began to cry. I was totally overcome by His love for me, and His desire to just walk and talk and share His life with me.

For the next two hours we sang love songs—secular love songs—to each other...

"Please Help Me, I'm Falling in Love with You"

"I Can't Help Falling in Love with You"

"I Have Often Walked Down this Street Before"

"Love, Love Me Do"

And, many others.

We walked in the forest, and we ran, and danced, and had fun together. And at the end of my "siesta," I knew as I had never known before how much He loved me, and how much I loved Him. And now I was free like never before to tell Him so.

In the past I have taught on intimacy with the Lord, I have preached on the "Song of Songs," but never before had I sensed such a closeness and a physical love for Jesus.

I have always felt that it is easier for a woman, than for a man to love the Lord in an intimate sense, and so I asked Him how men could "fall in love" with Him.

"Well," He replied, "You just did all that with a lion, and not with a man!"

I had not been aware of His form, but of course, yes! I had just been running in the forest with a Lion! He suggested to me that a lot of men find it easier to love their pets than their wives, but I think He had tongue-in-cheek when He said it! Some men that I have shared all this with agree that they like the idea of loving a lion, rather than loving the man, Jesus! Of course, the Lord is capable of revealing Himself in whatever way He feels is best for each of us, and we must just show Him that we want to love Him and leave the rest up to Him!

He had been right, of course, that it was much more refreshing to go out with Him than to sleep. I felt better than I had for a long time, and I was so grateful for all He was allowing me to experience. But I had seen nothing yet!

CHAPTER 7

The First Journey

The following day I was settling down for my siesta when the Lord began singing again, "Come fly with Me..."

I laughed, and when He gave me the choice of going out with Him or going to sleep, I knew I wanted the adventure with Him.

I didn't know then that He had chosen His song especially because He was going to take me flying! Each day for the next two weeks He came to invite me out when I was settling down to doze in the afternoon. Each time He gave me the choice of sleeping or flying somewhere with Him!

Well, which would you choose?

Suddenly, I was riding on the back of the Lion of Judah, and we were flying through the air and going down towards Northern Italy. This was to be the first of many visits to different places all over the world, but I didn't know that at the time. The Lion of Judah was my constant traveling companion, and He remained as the Lion except for a couple of times when He did a quick "DNA change" and became a man.

I have no idea, still today, if the places I visited exist or not, and I don't know if their geographical position is important. I feel that a lot of the places I saw could be anywhere in the world although some obviously couldn't, and I leave it to the discernment of the reader and the revelation of the Lord if He wants us to understand more. Here, I am just writing what I saw and experienced.

We arrived at our destination, which I believe was in Northern Italy, where we were in a small hall with an audience. In front of the people there was a magician performing great magic tricks. He was standing at the side of a small square table with golden ropes around it, and a cushion in the middle, and as he waved his magic wand and said the magic words, things appeared on the cushion. There was a crown, a rabbit, and a scantily dressed woman. The audience was amazed of course, and the magician was bowing and accepting with pleasure, the applause of his audience. The Lord said, "See, the devil understands the creative power available!"

Read the story of Simon the Sorcerer! (See Acts 8:9-25.)

He then took me to a small church. I don't know how I knew it was a church, I just did. It was not a traditional church building, but more like a meeting hall. There were about 100 people, and the pastor was on his knees in worship in front of the platform, while the congregation was all singing beautiful worship songs. Each one was totally lost in adoration of the Lord. On the platform there was a table similar to the one in the previous scene with the magician. As the pastor prayed, body parts began to appear in front of him (in much the same way the magician had produced things, but this time there were no magic words or wand waving)!

The pastor would say, "There is a heart here," and whoever in the congregation had need of a new heart would just fall out in the spirit as they received it. But the whole of the rest of the congregation just continued praising God. The service continued with different body parts appearing: kidneys and lungs, bones and joints, eyes and ears.

In the air over the people I could see lots of the DNA like I had seen in the first vision of the spirals leaving my bedroom wall, and I knew it was present in a concentrated form because of the praise of the people. The Lord told me that healing is good, but replacement parts are better. In the same way, you can repair a car engine, but it's better to have a new one than a reconditioned one!

He showed me that one of the keys to the success in allowing the Lord to do creative miracles was a humble pastor. I couldn't see his face, in total contrast to the magician who wanted to be known and recognized.

Another important factor was a unity in worship. No one was there to see what God might do, or even to hear a good sermon, but rather they had gathered with the sole intention of praising and worshipping Him—and that is what they were doing. No one was interested in the miracles happening. In fact, they seemed to not even notice, but were totally "lost in worship, love, and praise."

How we need to learn to focus on the Lord and not be distracted by the blessings that others are receiving.

CHAPTER 8

Picnics

Another day, the Lord took me to a clearing in a forest in Austria. When we arrived it was a party atmosphere—there was music playing, and there were woodland animals mingling with the adults and children at an enormous picnic table. I didn't mind the animals, but found it strange that they should be there, and I felt as though I had become part of a fairy story or Disney film! The Lord said it was because here, they put their emphasis on a Creator God, and that's why they were outside, and why the animals were a part of the church!

I was not convinced it was a Christian church because it all looked a bit "New Age" to me, so I pressed the Lord for further reassurance. He assured me it was fine and said, "Watch this."

He then went and sat at the foot of a cross in the center of the clearing (I hadn't noticed the cross before). Within a few seconds, the music stopped, there was an awesome silence, and everyone, including the animals were kneeling around the cross in a large circle. Obviously everyone had sensed His presence, but I don't know if they could see Him or not. I don't know how long the silence lasted either, but later there was worship and then more feasting!

As I reflect on this experience now, I am sad at how often I have judged by first impressions, and only seen a part of what was there. I hadn't seen the cross until the Lord pointed it out to me. I had been distracted by what I didn't like, and that had stopped me from seeing the heart of this community.

Oh Lord, open our spiritual eyes to see what You would have us see!

The Lion said to me later that there is no hierarchy in this church, "They just worship Me as King, and My Father as Creator!" I was aware of how I had judged by my first impression, and knew that the Lord was teaching me not to do that. He likes every style of church where the heart is right, and where He is given the praise and glory. Far too often I have visited churches and judged them by what I have seen, instead of "seeing" in the Spirit!

The next day we went to another "picnicking" church, but this time we didn't stay to eat with them! This one was in Northern Germany. It was a small (about 100 people), traditional style church with no central aisle, a block of pews in the middle, two side aisles, and a block of pews against the two side walls. It had an air of being well cared for. The pews were very old and well polished, and the brass candlesticks glowed with years of polishing. As we entered at the door in the back, the air was full of beautiful music, like old-fashioned chants—no instruments, just voices. I'm still not sure if this was a modern day church or one from the middle-ages! I had tried to see what the people were wearing, but I can't be sure. I do, however, know that lots of the women were wearing long dresses, but I don't know about the men. I guess that it is not important or the Lord would confirm it to me.

Jesus walked round the church and I stayed by His side. Everyone had their eyes closed and was in an attitude of worship. As we continued several times slowly walking round the church, the chants died away, and an awesome silence fell just as it had in the Austrian forest, and I knew the Lord was meeting the deepest needs of the people. One or two fell to their knees or to their seats, but most just stayed lost in love and worship.

The Lord explained to me that the chant they had been singing was simply, *"Come, Jesus, Come,"* and that He had no option but to come because they would not go home until He had visited them. That's when He showed me their picnic baskets, which were all in a back room of the church, saying that they had come prepared to stay all day waiting for Him to arrive in power and tangible presence.

What a lesson for those of us who try to force our church services into one and one-half or two hour slots on a Sunday morning. How much do we really want Him to visit with us? Are we prepared to stay all day?

As we left, the Lord told me that this small church had worked very hard towards unity. They had at one time, had a lot of divisions, but they had decided as individuals, they wanted Jesus to be the Lord of their lives and of their church. They had worked from there and He, Jesus, had done the rest!

"How good and pleasant it is when brothers live together in unity!"—Psalm 133:1

CHAPTER 9

The Igloo Church

On the next outing, I rode once more on the back of the Lion, and we flew to Greenland. We arrived and I could see nothing but snow, and then suddenly we met a dog-sleigh with a family in it on their way to church. The Lion ran along side and we "raced" them until we arrived, all of us laughing a lot as we went. What fun it is to do things with the Lord!

There was a very friendly atmosphere in the church, which was inside a huge igloo. As people arrived they were served a hot, spiced wine. The Lion and I stood in a corner and watched people welcoming each other. One man arrived and said, "Oh, it's so good to be here. You can sense the presence of the Lord already." I was pleased and said so to the Lion, as I gave Him an encouraging "dig" with my elbow.

Then He said, "But they don't know I'm here! They don't know Me at all. They have learned some of the language of 'Church,' but the pleasure they feel is as much for the warm drink and for each other as for Me. But they will know Me before long. They keep being drawn back here, and they have a great love for each other."

He explained that it was His Spirit which was attracting them to church, but so far they had not really recognized Him or His power among them. Later, He told me that even in the sleigh race on the way to the Igloo Church, the other family had not seen us. They had felt an exhilaration drawing them along, but they didn't know it was the Lord. He went on to say that they would recognize Him before long because He was about to reveal Himself to them! Lord, give us all a spirit of wisdom and revelation in the knowledge of You!

"I keep asking that the God of our Lord Jesus Christ, the glorious Father, may give you the Spirit of wisdom and revelation, so that you may know Him better."—Ephesians 1:17

As the service began and they started to sing, the Lion did a "quick DNA change" and became Jesus the King, dressed in green and golden robes. He went and stood by the cross at the front of the church for a while, and then He moved around the congregation. This time I didn't walk with Him, but stayed in a corner watching everything. I could tell who could sense His presence, and it looked to me as though some were looking straight at Him. He said that they hadn't seen Him, but they would!

He was always very reassuring, and wherever we went, even when things were not as they should be, He would always be positive about the future, and He knew what He was going to do to put things right. He is purifying His Church.

"...to purify for Himself a people that are His very own, eager to do what is good."—Titus 2:14

CHAPTER 10

Across the World

The next church we visited was in Mexico, where over 200 people have been raised from the dead. The Lord told me that fact on the way there, and in my naiveté I fully expected to see a newly dead person waiting to be raised! But no, it was a big praise party with people of every age singing and dancing. There was no children's ministry going on at that time, everyone was in together, and everyone was praising Him. I could see lots and lots of spirals of DNA in the atmosphere, and the Lord told me that in this church they could get what they wanted from Him because they believed His Word. They believed that God had spoken life into nothingness at the beginning of time, and in many of their personal stories, they had seen their own lives resurrected from nothing. And, God was getting all the Glory!

I saw no miracles, but I enjoyed the praise, and obviously the Lord did too.

In Central Australia, we went to an Amish-style church. It was Sunday evening, and the workers from the farming community were all gathered in the main house for worship. There was a middle-aged lady playing a piano—it felt homey, honest, and good. It reminded me of something from an old cowboy film. The Lord told me that these people have been protected from a lot of worldly contamination, and consequently hadn't learned much about spiritual warfare, but that it was okay. He could see that I would have thought they needed to learn about lots of things they had missed. He then explained to me that their life was about looking after sheep and cattle, and as a result, they understand about The Good Shepherd who looks after His sheep. They were faithful to Him and expect Him to meet their needs—and of course He does!

"...The LORD is my shepherd, I shall not be in want."—Psalm 23:1

On another journey, another day, we went to Southern India, to a western-style church which had been built by missionaries over a hundred years ago. It had a small steeple and long church-style windows, and was built of grey stone. It looked strange to me in the middle of the huts of the Indian village, and would have been much more in place on a village green somewhere in the English countryside. I was saddened by the thought that far too often, and for too long, missionaries went from Europe and took "westernized" Christianity to the rest of the world! But the Lord didn't comment on my thoughts, and it didn't seem to bother Him.

As we arrived, I became aware that the village was empty, and every single person from there was in church. The Lion was very pleased with this church, and before we went into the service He ran round the building several times leaping and dancing with joy—making me laugh! He was rejoicing in their praise which we could hear through the open door and windows. He told me these villagers have seen resurrection life and abundant life come out of the darkness of what they had before they began to believe His word.

When we entered, I saw a lot of DNA in the air, and everyone was worshipping. I stood at the back and watched as the Lion walked through the congregation. After awhile it became evident that He was dividing them into small groups of four or five, which then started praying together. Later the groups left one-by-one to go off to evangelize the surrounding villages. It was important that they had waited for His empowering before going off on their missionary journeys. I knew how sad the Lord was that too often we have set off on our own projects without waiting for His Spirit to be our guide.

CHAPTER 11

The Roaring Lion

The place we visited in Pakistan was a larger house in a small town—a house with many entrances. Women arrived at all times of the day, stayed for as long as they could, anything from ten minutes to an hour or more, and then they left by a different entrance. It was important that they were not followed, or seen to be coming to a Christian meeting. There were a few men, but not many in the service which was continuous worship, praise, and Bible study—24 hours a day. It was led by a small devoted group of missionaries who had prayed hard to find a way to meet the needs of the people, and share the gospel with them. They were giving a great sacrifice in time and effort, keeping their church open round-the-clock.

I saw how much the Lord appreciated them and wanted to encourage them, and while He didn't move,

I knew that He was blessing each one as they came and went. I stood at the back of the room with the Lion and we watched people coming and going. We listened to some prayers and some praise. There was only a single musician, and some teaching, and then suddenly without any warning, and without really moving, the Lion roared! The only explanation I got for His roaring was, "Because this was War!"

When the book of Joel talks about the last days, he talks about the judgment of the nations, and prophesies:

"The Lord will roar from Zion, and thunder from Jerusalem; the earth and sky will tremble. But the Lord will be a refuge for His people, a stronghold for the people of Israel."—Joel 3:16

I believe what I heard was a roar against the nations, as well as the Lord verifying that this place was a refuge for His people whom He is gathering out of the "nations." There was no visible effect on the gathering of people there, as though they hadn't heard His roar, so I supposed it was just a roar in the Spirit.

Knowing something had happened in the spiritual realm, the Lord told me that the women visiting this house were either Muslim or Hindu, and had to come in secret. That's why they came and left through different doorways. But that each of them would bring their families to the Lord before too long.

Only in one other place did the Lion roar, and that was in, Singapore. We arrived at what was a very large building with no seats, and a lot of people milling around. Maybe it was a market hall or something? At least that's what I thought at first, but then I realized everyone was moving in a sort of formation: three or four steps to the left, and then the same back to the right, all the time edging forward from one wall to the opposite one, and back again—most appearing to be mumbling to themselves. I later learned that they were praying in the Spirit. There was no acknowledgement of each other, but everyone was totally absorbed in what they were doing.

The Lord explained to me that they were moving in the way that a Chinese dragon would move in a carnival. This building used to be a Buddhist temple and they were reclaiming it for the Lord. They knew they had to repeatedly cover every inch of the ground and pray for a certain length of time each time they met until the place was totally cleansed, and the Spirit would tell them when it was done.

I don't know how long it went on for, but eventually a worship group started somewhere, although I didn't see them (in fact I never saw any worship leaders and I felt as though this was because of humility on their part). Slowly the people stopped moving and praying and started to worship. I didn't really like the Chinese music but the Lord loved it because it came from their heart. Before long, everyone was united in worship and the Lord told me there was great unity of purpose to see

His name lifted high in their country, and to see Buddha under their feet. I felt as though the Lion was going to speak or something, but nothing else happened. I was learning to wait and watch.

Before long, I was back in my hospital bed, but I knew in my spirit that something was happening in Singapore, and maybe I'd be able to see the next thing another time.

It was the following afternoon, in real time, when this vision came back to me. I was suddenly once more immersed in the worship with them, and that's when the Lion roared the loudest roar I have ever heard. It was both deafening and awesome, and much, much louder than the roar I had heard in Pakistan. Immediately, everyone was flat on their faces, and the roar was echoing round the walls. Then there was a silence, a really thick, solid silence, such as can only be felt after such an incredibly loud noise!

Two hours later (in my time), the picture returned once more and there was still the same deafening silence, but people were just beginning to move. Slowly they got up, the worship group started again, and everyone began praising the Lord. The Lord said to me, "It's okay. It's done, we can go now. They'll get up and have a praise party and a lot of people will now come into Christianity from Buddhism. The job is finished!"

There are several references in the Bible to the roaring Lion. I've already mentioned one in Joel. Here I would like to remind the reader of two others.

THE ROARING LION

"...[The Lord] will roar like a lion. When He roars, His children will come trembling from the west. They will come trembling like birds from Egypt, like doves from Assyria. 'I will settle them in their homes,' declares the Lord."—Hosea 11:10-11

I believe that "His children" in this verse means, all those whom the Lord is calling into His Kingdom to be a part of the end time harvest.

The other verse I want to quote is a wonderful passage from Job, and needs no comments from me, it just asks us to meditate on it!

"Listen! Listen to the roar of His voice, to the rumbling that comes from His mouth. He unleashes His lightning beneath the whole heaven and sends it to the ends of the earth. After that comes the sound of His roar; He thunders with His majestic voice. When His voice resounds He holds nothing back. God's voice thunders in marvelous ways; He does great things beyond our understanding."—Job 37:2-5

CHAPTER 12

Non-Christian Gatherings

In contrast to the Singapore church, which had previously been a Buddhist temple in Jakarta, we visited a place which was still dedicated to Buddha. The first thing I saw there was a huge statue of Buddha twenty-times the size of a man. Many people were sitting cross-legged on the floor meditating. They were totally absorbed in what they were doing, and no one took any notice of us.

The Lion was more tense than I had ever seen Him as we walked together all round the outside wall inside of the building. The walls were lined with intricately carved wood, but I didn't take much notice of the details, I was too intent in staying with the Lion and watching Him. I knew we were on enemy territory. He was growling quietly all the time, as if daring any of the enemy spirits to come near. He told me that He has the right to be there, for two reasons. First, because He is the Sovereign Lord, and the world does in-fact belong to Him! Second, because of all the Christian tourists and missionaries over the years who have visited this place and prayed. They have prayed for the people who are so deceived, prayed for those who are really searching, and prayed for an entry for Him, so that this temple would become the home of the Living God, and Christ would be revealed here. What I was witnessing was the beginning of the fulfillment of the prayers of many generations!

After the tour of the room, the Lion left me at the back, and I watched as He began to walk among the people, licking some, breathing on some, and brushing up against others. He told me that these were the ones who were genuinely searching and He was drawing them to Himself. Each day He draws them closer, and many of them will come to know Him over the next year. The time is short, and we will see the beginning of the final harvest very soon.

The other non-Christian place the Lord took me to was a Jewish synagogue in Israel. The meeting was full, and I was on the balcony surrounded by many women and children. The man at the front was reading from Isaiah 61:

"The Spirit of the Sovereign Lord is upon me..."

When he put down the scroll, I looked hard to see if it was Jesus, but it wasn't. I didn't see the Lord anywhere in this picture, but I knew He had taken me there and left me for some reason. The reader put down the scroll and then said to the congregation, "This is one of the prophecies for the Messiah, and I believe we are in such troubled times at the moment in our country, and all over the world, that we need to be looking forward to the coming of the Messiah. I want to challenge you this week to read the scriptures and find as many references as you can to the coming King of Israel."

I then saw two women chatting in the balcony; both of them had young children with them. One turned to the other and said, "They could well end up finding Jesus of Nazareth!"

The other replied, "Exactly! My cousin has just become a Christian and joined a group of Messianic Jews!"

The first said, "My nephew is trying to do the same, and it is causing chaos in our family!"

I was excited, and knew that the Lord has never, for a minute, given up on His chosen people, and that the scales are being taken from their eyes so that many can come into the Kingdom and find salvation in the name of Jesus.

We must continue to pray for Israel.

CHAPTER 13

The Pride Problem

We went next to a large wooden chalet in Denmark, and when we entered, the people were singing worship songs, but it wasn't worship. It bothered me because I could tell that the singing was not coming from their hearts! The Lord said, "There is no unity here, but it will come." He is always positive about the future.

I saw some individuals, who were worshipping, and I saw those who were definitely not—they had their eyes open, were not singing, and had a cold expression on their faces. Others were *pretending*—they had their eyes closed and were singing, but I could see that their hearts were cold.

The Lord showed me the problems in this church. The first was one of the leadership team. There were six on the pastoral team, and all were faceless except one. (During the visions I had come to realize that if

I couldn't see the face of the pastors or of the worship leaders it means that they are humble people and not taking glory for themselves, but giving it all to the Lord.) The one face I could see was a woman pastor who was manipulative, dominant, and proud.

The second problem was that certain of the older elders of the church were not wanting to flow with the Lord, but they too, like the pastor, were proud of their own achievements, and had their own agenda. (I did not sense that there is any problem with either female pastors, or older elders, but there is a problem with all who are proud, dominant, and who want to follow their own agenda!)

The scene changed, and it was as though I was watching a cartoon film of the same building, but now we were on the outside of it, and there was obviously a big party going on inside. There was a lot of noise and light coming from each window and also through the splits in the roof, which were caused when the building bounced to the music! The elders of the church were all holding strong ropes to try to hold the building down and stop it from flying away.

As we watched, the female pastor was ejected through the roof, and then the Lion walked round and either cut the ropes, or He put a paw on the heads of the elders so that they melted. He was getting rid of all the bad influences, and I knew that it was in answer to prayer of the few real worshipping members of the church. The only thing they had needed to do was pray and leave it to the Lord who was doing it in the best way—His way.

Next, the scene changed again and we were in another service. The pastoral team, without the woman I had seen ejected, was standing at the front of the church. One leader said that none of the pastors had received a message for this morning's service, so they were just going to sit in silence and listen to what the Lord might be saying. I knew that this would not have been allowed to happen if the 'proud pastor' had still been there. She would have had to have everything planned for each service! There would also have been an outcry from the elders who wanted the service to be always organized and planned.

We waited for quite awhile, and then one of the old "lead weight" elders stood and started to cry, saying that he had to repent of many things. I didn't hear any of his confession, because the Lion turned to me and said, "It's okay for us to leave now. The changes have begun."

Later, when I was thinking of this church, the Lord showed me a verse which seemed appropriate:

"In those days Israel had no king; everyone did as he saw fit."—Judges 21:25

I knew that a church which doesn't have unity, doesn't have the King. And those who don't know the King, do as they think fit, or what seems right to them. How sad that is! His agenda is so much more interesting and exciting than ours.

CHAPTER 14

Walking and Dancing

In central West Africa, the Lord and I joined people walking along a road. This time it felt as though He was just a normal man and not a Lion or a King! Many of these people walked for two hours or more to go to church, and I think they must often experience the Lord walking beside them as in the Emmaus road story (see Luke 24:13-17).

The church was in the open air, and people came and left as they wanted to, or were able. I participated in the praise and listened to the teaching, both of which went on for a long time. If people are going to spend two hours on the road, the church meeting has to be longer than an hour! The Lord told me that these people often have meetings which last all day. Here again, there was no time limit, and people brought food to share. The Lord pointed out to me a man in the congregation saying that he used to be a witch doctor, but that these people had convinced him of the truth of Christ.

"They overcame him by the blood of the Lamb and by the word of their testimony."—Revelation 12:11

I knew that he was not the only example of people there being reclaimed from the enemy camp, and I praised the Lord that He always has the victory!

The last church I visited was in Holland. We went to the very north of the Netherlands to a service which was taking place in a windmill. There were about 50 people all sitting on hard wooden benches. But as I looked up into the mechanism of the windmill sails, I could see there were several angels smiling down and looking very happy to be there.

As the service started and someone was speaking at the front, several people fell asleep. I laughingly pointed out the sleeping people to the Lord, but He said it was okay.

"These people are very tired," He explained. "Because they work very hard and life is not easy for them, but they are faithful to Me and rarely miss church, even if they are very tired."

He walked round and breathed on the sleeping ones so that they woke. Then starting at the back, He walked between each row of people, and I noticed that He was specifically stepping on their feet. Before He arrived at the front of the church, the back row was dancing. And soon we were all dancing, but there wasn't enough room in the church so we danced outside. And when I looked up, the angels I had seen inside were swinging on the sails of the windmill!

We danced for a long time and then people danced away towards their homes, and we were singing the song based on Isaiah 55:12:

"You will go out in joy, and be led forth in peace; and the mountains and hills will burst into song before you, and all the trees of the field will clap their hands."

I was suddenly hoping to hear "the trees of the field clap their hands," but in this part of Holland there are few trees, so there were none in my vision! I expressed my disappointment to the Lord and He pointed out to me that all the grasses and the tall reeds were moving to the music. I knew that creation was singing and dancing with us.

I watched people dancing away and it was only then that I realized the people were all wearing traditional Dutch costumes! It was a beautiful sight and remains etched on my memory. If I could paint, it would be one of the things I would like to try to put onto canvas.

CHAPTER 15

More About Annonay

From my hospital bed I could see nothing but the sky! In the long nights I used to watch the passage of the stars or the moon, and I began to know why people are attracted to study astronomy or write stories and poems about life on another planet, or why they would want to fly! For my part, I praised the God of the universe for His amazing creation, and tried to remember some of the Bible verses I knew about the heavens, singing many songs in praise of creation.

"The heavens declare the glory of God, the skies proclaim the work of His hands. Day after day they pour forth speech; night after night they display knowledge."—Psalm 19:1-2

I really felt the heavens were speaking back to me and showing me a steadfast, faithful Creator, who really does hold the world in His hands.

Because the hospital is on the top of one of the hills in this mountainous region, and almost everything else is down in the valley, or at least lower down the hillside than the hospital, I spent much time contemplating the heavens.

Once I was finally able to get out of bed and sit in a chair, then I could see across the valley and look down over the rooftops. There seemed to be a lot of churches or church schools, because many of the buildings looked to have a cross on the top. When I had a visit from a local pastor, we talked about it.

Before my husband had left me in the hospital and returned home to spend the New Year's celebrations with our family near Paris, he had telephoned a local pastor whose name he found on a hospital list. Unfortunately there was no reply, but Malgwyn left a message and just prayed that there would be a response. He really was not too happy about leaving me in the state I was in, and he was afraid I would be lonely!

Well the pastor responded very quickly and visited me the following day. Unfortunately, at that time, I was too ill to talk much, but he came again when I was recovering. Together we talked about what God is doing in different parts of the world, and we prayed together about many things, although I did not tell him about any of my visions or travels with the Lord. They were all too new to me, and I needed time to reflect on them.

This pastor also asked a member of his church to visit me. Nicole (not her real name) was a blessing and a joy to me, and we have exchanged letters ever since I came home. These two dear people were the only visitors I had during my three week stay, so they were very welcome and I was more than happy to see them. The hospital staff was also all very nice, and I spent a lot of time talking to them as their schedules allowed. I remember especially the two physiotherapists. They were both blind! One blind physiotherapist didn't surprise me, but when the second one arrived I thought it was quite strange. They were both very interesting men, we talked a lot about many things, and I still pray for them both when I think about my time in Annonay.

From the staff, but more from my two new Christian friends, I learned that the area had suffered greatly because of religious wars in the past, and a lot of blood had been shed as Protestants and Catholics had fought to the death.

"Lord, forgive us for the things we've done in Your Name that were not of You."

I was thinking about these things one day when the Lion decided to take me on a tour of the town of Annonay. I was very pleased, because I had arrived in Annonay in the middle of the night and so had seen nothing, and I knew that when the day came for me to go back to the north by ambulance, I was probably going to leave very early in the morning, so again I would see nothing.

I rode, for the most part, on the back of the Lion, and we went down into the valley, and up and down the winding roads. He brushed His mane along the side or the corner of several buildings and I knew that He was purifying them or marking them for Himself. We visited several schools and He breathed long, hard breaths in through the doorways or gates. He did the same in the churches that we saw, and I now know that His Spirit is revealing Himself to these congregations. Before we returned to the hospital, we walked over a bridge and I stood and looked down into the river while the Lion put one of His huge paws into the water. It was as if the river turned to blood, and I knew that it was His blood that had been shed for forgiveness, and that He was purifying the area of the bad things of the past.

Every year the town of Annonay has a festival when they celebrate the Montgolfier brothers who invented the hot air balloon. I thought it was one of those strange things that the Lord should put me in a hospital in the place where man had begun to fly, and then take me flying Himself, all over the world. I'm sure there is significance there, and I pray for the town of Annonay, that the Holy Spirit will give a spiritual thirst to many in the town and then reveal Himself to all who seek Him. I pray, too, that they will learn to "fly" with Him.

"...Those who hope in the Lord will renew their strength. They will soar on wings like eagles; they will run and not grow weary, they will walk and not faint."—Isaiah 40:31

CHAPTER 16

The "Whys and Wherefores"

I have questioned the Lord since I came home from the hospital, about why He should show me all these things, and why I should be so privileged to travel the world with Him! In reply, He told me that just as any man would tell his fiancée about the work he does during the day, He was showing me what He is doing. Once more, just in His reply, He was reminding me of His love for me, and that we are engaged to be married, and one day soon I shall be a part of the whole Church which will be His Bride!

I do not believe I have exclusivity on the visions that I had, you can have them too. You have to pray for the Lord to speak to you and reveal Himself to you, and then give Him freedom and time to do it! I must add that I believe there is a danger in seeking voices and visions! If our hearts are not totally committed to the Lord, the enemy could have an entry point and he is all too ready to cooperate with visions and dreams that lead to destruction! So my advice is to seek the Lord Himself and have the desire to know Him better, and let Him reveal Himself to you in the way He chooses!

So what did I learn about what He is doing in my own life as well as around the world?

I have tried to sum up what I experienced and what I saw, and I'm sure there are many more things still to come out of it. As I think of them and remember them, I get new revelations. I do not believe it was a one-off experience, and I expect the Lord to show me more as our relationship gets deeper, and as I get more and more impatient for His return.

There are several points I feel can be used to generalize what I learned:

• In places where He is not known He is drawing people to Himself, and revealing Himself to those who are genuinely searching. The fact that people are members of other religions is no barrier to the Lord revealing Himself, and we need to be praying for people to seek the truth with all their hearts—because we know that He is the Truth.

"You will seek Me and find Me when you seek Me with all your heart."—Jeremiah 29:13

• Where there is no unity in His Church, He is bringing unity by melting hard hearts and moving out those who refuse to change. We need to pray for His will to be done in all the places meeting in His name. Purify Your Church, Lord (see Malachi 3:2-5).

• Where there is unity, He is enjoying it, and bringing many blessings and miracles. We need to pray for more of it and praise Him more, and more.

"Again, I tell you that if two of you on earth agree about anything you ask for, it will be done for you by My Father in Heaven. For where two or three come together in My name, there am I with them."
—Matthew 18:19-20

I saw the common factors in the churches which pleased Him most, where He had freedom to do what He wanted and to meet the needs of the people. These factors were as follows:

• They believed the whole of the Bible.

• They arrived at church with no personal agenda, but just intent on worshipping.

• They came prepared to stay all day, and often expected to stay all day.

• They often ate together.

• They had extended times of praise and worship.

• The pastors and the worship leaders were "faceless."

They were humble people wanting only to serve the Lord.

I learned of how He cares for the dying, and won't let them go until they see Him! We need to pray for people to recognize Him as He reveals Himself to them.

"I keep asking that the God of our Lord Jesus Christ, the glorious Father, may give you the Spirit of wisdom and revelation, so that you may know Him better." —Ephesians1:17

I learned to laugh and to cry with Him, but most important of all I learned to love Him passionately, and I learned just how much He desperately wants to spend time with me, not working together, but just enjoying each other and being together.

I am now more convinced than ever that whatever is happening anywhere in my life, in my country, in my church, and in the world, the Lord knows it and is dealing with it, so it's okay. This does not mean that we are let off the hook as far as prayer is concerned. In fact, the contrary is true. Much of what I saw happening was as a result of fervent prayer over the years. Christians today have a responsibility to pray for His will to be done in every situation, in every area of the globe.

Everything I saw was an encouragement to me, and a revelation of just how positive the Lord Himself is about everything—even where things might look depressing to us and seem to be not going totally His way for the moment—at least from our point of view. He sees the future and knows the end of the story!

We must pray for people to seek Him and then He will be found by them. We must discover afresh how much He loves us and wants us to love Him. The praise and worship we give Him from our hearts increases the presence of the creative power in the DNA and gives Him freedom to do what He wants in our own lives and those of others. Jesus is coming back and we can help that time to advance or we can hinder it. The choice is ours!

He is preparing His harvest all over the world —Hallelujah!

CHAPTER 17

The Working Christian

One of the times I was relaxing with Him, the Lord gave me a drama to perform. It speaks of Christians working and working, and spending so little time with Him. It was one of the lessons I had to learn, but I know it is for others too. I will write it below. Please feel free to use it in your own churches or groups if it speaks to your situation.

Christian awakens and prays in "automatic mode." It's obviously a habit!

Christian: Good morning, Lord. Thank you for a good night's sleep, please be with me in all I do today. I have lots of gospel seeds to plant for You, Lord. Please bless them and keep me strong as I work for You. Amen.

Christian is working, digging the earth in order to plant his gospel seeds.

Jesus is a voice from off stage.

Jesus: Christian, come let's have fun together!

Christian: Oh Lord, thank You for being here, I need Your strength.

Christian continues with his digging and planting.

Jesus: Christian, come let's walk together.

Christian: Oh no, Lord. You know that I have so much to do. Your just being here strengthens me. Thank You so much!

He continues digging once more, mopping his brow and obviously getting tired.

Jesus: Christian, come let's run together!

Christian: Lord, this ground is so difficult. Thank You for being here and helping. We'll get it all done if we work together, won't we Lord?

He continues working, but slowly now, and with great determination.

Jesus: Christian, let's fly together!

Christian: Later Lord, later. All I ask is that You help me plant these seeds of the gospel for You.

That night, Christian is going to bed and he kneels by his bed to pray.

Christian: Thank You, Lord, for Your presence and Your help today—I couldn't do it alone. I am so grateful that You were with me and encouraged me. In fact, it seemed today that You were closer than normal, almost as though I could really hear Your voice!

Please strengthen me as I sleep tonight, so that I can do the same work again tomorrow.

Jesus: But Christian, if you had come with Me, we could have flown together, and you could have sown your seeds from a great height where the Holy Spirit would have carried them and planted them in good soil, in ground that I have already prepared. And if you had flown with Me you would have been refreshed and renewed, and not so tired now.

Ah well, maybe tomorrow!

Chapter 18

The Last Word

(Added by my husband, Malgwyn Elmer)

For many years now, Anne and I have always shared our Christian experiences. For the most part we have done things together, or we have discussed and planned things before doing them. Because of work commitments, I have usually been several steps behind Anne in my journey with the Lord, but that has not stopped us from having a strong sense of unity together with Jesus. This was the first time in several years that we had experienced a long period of "forced separation," and I know that Anne was a bit wary of my reaction when she started to tell me about her visions and her travels.

One particular weekend stands out in my memory; it was to be my first visit to Anne in the hospital since her travels with the Lion started. She hadn't told me about the Lion in our conversations over the telephone, only that she had had strange visions that were very important.

So it was with strong anticipation that I set off on the six hour drive to Annonay that Friday evening in January. On the way, I listened to some of my favorite worship cassettes, and then I put on the latest cassette that we had received from The Elijah List (www.elijahlist.com)—an internet ministry that distributes prophetic messages on the internet and by audio CD). I don't even remember the name of the speaker, but the message was about the way the Lord was moving in the greatest power in churches and communities where people were in complete unity in their wish to experience more of Him. It even mentioned the Lion of Judah, but I don't remember the context now. The places where miracles were occurring more and more regularly, including miracles of people receiving "spare parts" for defective organs, were places where people were not waiting for the "big names" to come and minister to them, or the well known worship leaders to come and lead the worship. These were unknown churches with "faceless" pastors where it didn't matter what denomination you were from—just *everyone* together, worshipping the Lord from their hearts. The common factors being: unity, faith, and an unwavering belief in the full gospel message.

It was too late for me to visit Anne that Friday night, but I was there as soon as possible on Saturday morning. Just before arriving at the hospital, I stopped off in the local shopping center and bought a Walkman so she could listen to this fantastic message.

As soon as I arrived, Anne's story came bubbling out at full speed. She started by saying something like, "I know you'll think I'm out of my mind, but this is what has been happening to me. Please just listen before you say I'm crazy." I couldn't believe how similar the message was to my cassette: unity, faceless pastors, worship from the heart, and no recognition of church denominations. I just kept interrupting and repeating, "You must listen to this cassette." When she finished her story, I sensed that she was a wee bit disappointed that I believed every word of her experiences and that I wasn't really surprised, because the Lord had confirmed the story to me in the message I had heard during my journey from home.

The Lord had honored our "togetherness," and had prepared my heart with the same message! What an amazing God we serve!

What about the fruit, to use a "churchy" term? Well Anne has definitely become more mellow and more peaceful. Her attitude towards other people and other churches with respect to their position within the Body of Christ has become even more, one of acceptance, than it was before. We have tried for many years to work for unity across denominations, but now we know like never before, that Jesus is aware of where people are, what they are thinking, and what they believe in their hearts. He is in control. He is working to unify and purify His church, and we just get blessed as we pray for the fulfillment of His will. Everyone will see Him in the end—Hallelujah!

To contact Anne and Malgwyn Elmer

Anne and her husband, Malgwyn, live in France where they are active in both French and English speaking Christian communities, and are both elders in L'Eglise Eau Vive, Boulogne-Billancourt on the outskirts of the city.

Originally from Lancashire, in the Northwest of England, they have three children and eleven grandchildren.

Since moving to France, in 1983, the Lord has led them into an open home policy, where many visitors from all over the world have benefited from their gift of hospitality.

Together they are praying–in a vision of running a Christian Conference Centre in the Paris region, and expect to see the fulfillment of this in the near future.

They can be contacted at:

Anne and Malgwyn Elmer
anne.elmer@editionsdelasource.fr

TRANSPORTED by the LION of JUDAH, has been translated and is available in French, German, Danish, Spanish, and Dutch. These versions can be obtained from:

Editions de la Source
www.editionsdelasource.com